This book
belongs to

....

....

Published in the United Kingdom
in 1446 AH (2025 CE) by
Learning Roots
Suite 15, Ideas House, Eastwood Close
London, E18 1BY
United Kingdom
www.learningroots.com

Copyright © Learning Roots 2025
Authored by Zaheer Khatri and Mariam Elgammal.
Quran translation by Dr Azhar Majothi.
Design and Illustrations by Jannah Haque, Fatima Zahur, Erika Gushiken and Daniela Montessi.

Acknowledgements
The publisher thanks Allah, Lord of the worlds, for making this publication possible.

Notice of Rights
All rights reserved. No part of this publication may be reproduced, stored in a retrieval system, or transmitted, in any form, or by any means, electronic, mechanical, photocopying, recording or otherwise without prior written permission from the publisher.

British Library Cataloguing in Publication Data
A CIP catalogue record for this book is available from the British Library.

Printed and bound in Türkiye.

First Edition
ISBN 978-1-915381-10-1

My First Surah Book

Introduction

Most children learn to recite the Quran, yet few learn to understand its meaning. We designed this book to allow children to benefit from the guidance of Allah's words by experiencing the meaning, power and guidance of the Quran first-hand.

With a selection of short Surahs in the Quran, we begin by exploring the story behind their revelation so children understand the context in which they were revealed. We then examine each Surah word by word to learn the translation and the meaning of the verses directly. The meanings have been made relatable to children from the works of famous tafsir books, such as Ibn Kathir.

Next, we internalise the meanings by posing a series of reflective questions that ask children to explore how the themes of the verses relate to their own lives.

By taking these short, simple, yet powerful steps, children experience the Quran on a whole new level and appreciate its beauty, energy and guidance, in-sha-Allah.

Chapters

The Opener
Surah al-Fatiha
Page 8

The Elephant
Surah al-Feel
Page 14

The Quraysh
Surah Quraysh
Page 20

Small Acts of Kindness
Surah al-Ma'oon
Page 26

The Heavenly River
Surah al-Kawther
Page 32

The Disbelievers
Surah al-Kafirun
Page 38

The Victory
Surah an-Nasr
Page 44

The Palm Fibre
Surah al-Masad
Page 50

Sincerity
Surah al-Ikhlas
Page 56

Daybreak
Surah al-Falaq
Page 62

Mankind
Surah an-Nas
Page 68

How to use this book

My First Surah Book is a wonderful learning experience that introduces children to the Surahs of the Quran through story, discovery and reflection. **kiitab** makes this book even better by reading out the chapters, word-for-word.

Find your way around easily with a clear layout.

Touch a word to hear its recital and translation.

Touch the star icon to hear a lesson explained.

Touch the search icon to play the 'Find Me Game'.

Touch a sentence to hear the explanation of a verse.

Touch an arrow to listen to the verse being recited.

Reflect on each Surah and listen to suggested thoughts.

Explore the story behind each Surah.

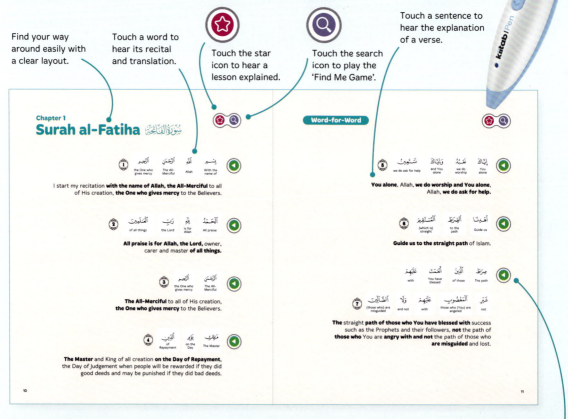

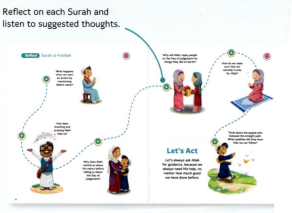

Meet

Zayd
Together, we'll learn to understand the Quran.

Nur
We'll uncover the story behind each Surah.

Deen
Let's discover the treasures of the Quran.

Yusuf
We'll reflect on what the Quran is telling us.

Sara
We'll make our lives better by following the Quran.

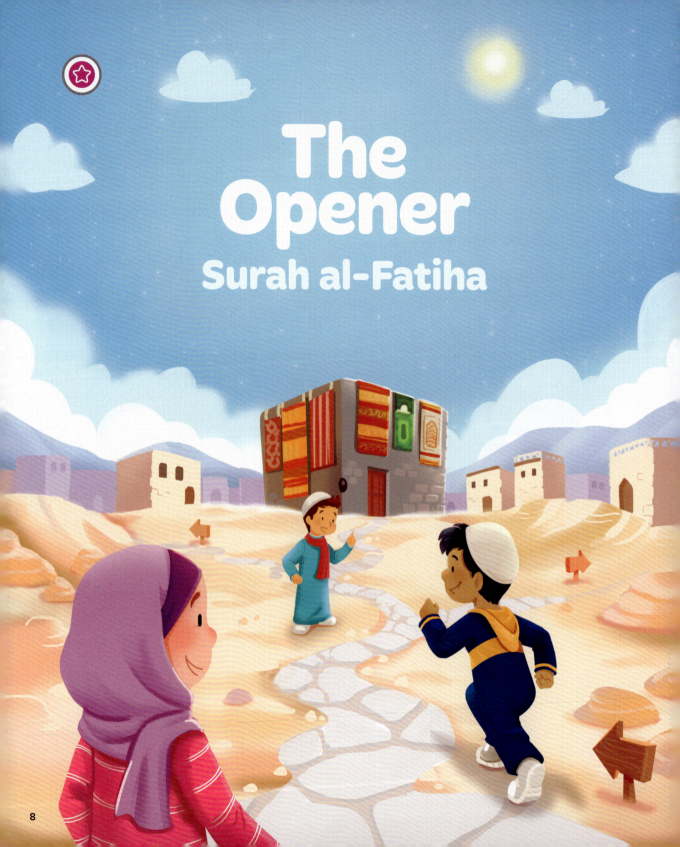

Introduction

"Shall I teach you the greatest Surah in the Quran before you leave the masjid?" Asked the Prophet ﷺ. He was speaking to Rafi bin al-Mu'alla, one of the Sahaba, or Companions of the Prophet ﷺ. Rafi had heard many beautiful verses, but to know the greatest Surah would be something special.

Before the Prophet ﷺ could tell Rafi, other Sahaba joined the gathering and began asking questions about Islam. Hours went by and Rafi noticed the Prophet ﷺ was getting ready to leave.

"O Messenger of Allah!" Rafi said. "You said you would teach me the greatest Surah in the Quran." The Prophet ﷺ smiled and took Rafi by the hand and began to recite a Surah that Rafi knew very well. It was Surah al-Fatiha. "These are the seven much-repeated verses," the Prophet ﷺ explained as Rafi listened closely. "And this Surah is part of the Glorious Quran given to me by Allah."

Let's discover the beautiful verses of this Surah and see what makes it the greatest Surah in the Quran.

Chapter 1
Surah al-Fatiha سُورَةُ الفَاتِحَةِ

1 | the One who gives mercy | The All-Merciful | Allah | With the name of

I start my recitation **with the name of Allah, the All-Merciful** to all of His creation, **the One who gives mercy** to the Believers.

2 | of all things | the Lord | is for Allah | All praise

All praise is for Allah, the Lord, owner, carer and master **of all things.**

3 | the One who gives mercy | The All-Merciful

The All-Merciful to all of His creation, **the One who gives mercy** to the Believers.

4 | of Repayment | on the Day | The Master

The Master and King of all creation **on the Day of Repayment,** the Day of Judgement when people will be rewarded if they did good deeds and may be punished if they did bad deeds.

Word-for-Word

5	نَسْتَعِينُ	وَإِيَّاكَ	نَعْبُدُ	إِيَّاكَ
	we do ask for help	and You alone	we do worship	You alone

You alone, Allah, **we do worship** and **You alone**, Allah, **we do ask for help**.

6	الْمُسْتَقِيمَ	الصِّرَاطَ	اهْدِنَا
	(which is) straight	to the path	Guide us

Guide us to the straight path of Islam.

عَلَيْهِمْ	أَنْعَمْتَ	الَّذِينَ	صِرَاطَ
with	You have blessed	of those	The path

7	الضَّالِّينَ	وَلَا	عَلَيْهِمْ	الْمَغْضُوبِ	غَيْرِ
	(those who) are misguided	and not	with	those who (You) are angered	not

The straight **path of those who You have blessed with** success, such as the Prophets and their followers, **not** the path of **those who** You are **angry with and not** the path of those who **are misguided** and lost.

11

Reflect Surah al-Fatiha

What happens when we start an action by mentioning Allah's name?

How does thanking and praising Allah help us?

Why does Allah remind us about His mercy before telling us about the Day of Judgement?

Why will Allah repay people on the Day of Judgement for things they did on Earth?

How do we make sure that our worship is only for Allah?

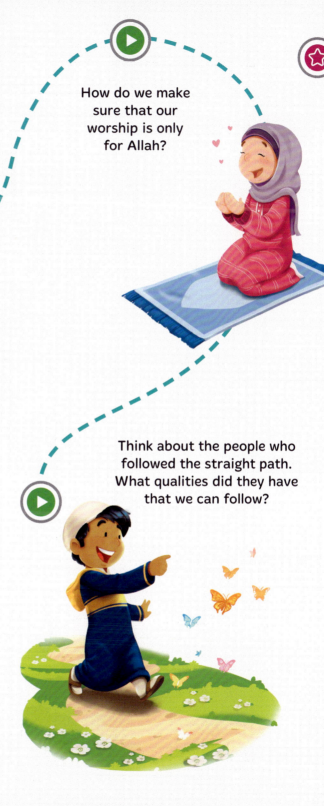

Think about the people who followed the straight path. What qualities did they have that we can follow?

Let's Act

Let's always ask Allah for guidance, because we always need His help, no matter how much good we have done before.

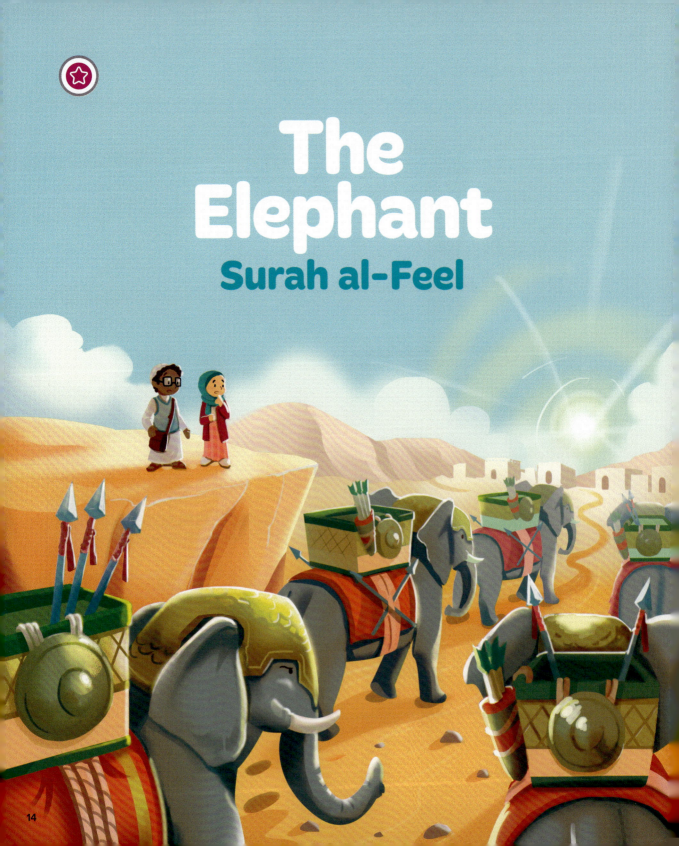

Introduction

The Prophet Muhammad ﷺ was born in a city called Makkah in the Year of the Elephant. This year was named after a famous event that the people of Makkah always remember. It all started with one man who had a terrible idea.

In a nearby land called Yemen, there ruled a powerful Christian king named Abraha. He was jealous that people chose to worship at the Ka'bah instead of his giant church. Abraha decided to destroy the Ka'bah. With a mighty army and enormous elephants, he marched towards Makkah, ready to carry out his wicked plan.

Fear quickly spread throughout the city of Makkah. The people had never faced an attack like this before. Would Abraha really be able to attack such a sacred place? What Abraha did not anticipate was that Allah had a bigger, mightier plan. He protected the Ka'bah in a way that no one could have imagined.

Let's explore the story of Surah al-Feel and discover the incredible way Allah defended His House.

Chapter 105
Surah al-Feel سُورَةُ الفِيلِ

الرَّحِيمِ	الرَّحْمَٰنِ	اللَّهِ	بِسْمِ
the One who gives mercy	The All-Merciful	Allah	With the name of

I start my recitation **with the name of Allah, the All-Merciful** to all of His creation, **the One who gives mercy** to the Believers.

①	الْفِيلِ	بِأَصْحَابِ	رَبُّكَ	فَعَلَ	كَيْفَ	تَرَ	أَلَمْ
	of the Elephant	to the Army	your Lord do	did	about what	you looked	Haven't

Haven't you looked and wondered **about what your Lord**, Allah, **did to the Army of the Elephant** led by Abraha when they tried to destroy the Ka'bah?

②	تَضْلِيلٍ	فِي	كَيْدَهُمْ	يَجْعَلْ	أَلَمْ
	not work out	to	their plan	He make	Didn't

Didn't He, Allah, **make their plan to** destroy the Ka'bah **not work out** as the army failed to march into Makkah?

③	أَبَابِيلَ	طَيْرًا	عَلَيْهِمْ	وَأَرْسَلَ
	in groups	birds	against them	And He sent

And He, Allah, **sent against them**, the army of Abraha, **birds** which flew **in groups**, one after another.

16

Word-for-Word

baked clay — made of — stones — They threw

They, the birds, **threw** down **stones made of baked clay** onto the army of Abraha.

eaten up — like stalks — And He made them

And this is how **He**, Allah, **made them,** the defeated army of Abraha, look **like** a field of **stalks** which had been **eaten up** by cattle and completely finished.

DID YOU KNOW?

While on their way to attack the Ka'bah, Abraha's army stole camels from Abdul Muttalib, the grandfather of the Prophet Muhammad ﷺ. Abdul Muttalib went to Abraha demanding his camels back. "Why do you only care for your camels? Aren't you worried about the Ka'bah?" Abraha said. Abdul Muttalib calmly replied, "I am the owner of the camels, and I have to protect them. But the Ka'bah has a different owner, its Lord will protect it!" And that's exactly what happened.

Reflect — Surah al-Feel

What does this Surah teach us about how Allah protects special things in Islam, such as the Ka'bah?

How does it make us feel to know that Allah's plan is better than the plan of others?

Allah sent small birds to stop Abraha's large army. What does that tell us about Allah's power?

What does this Surah teach us about how quickly Allah can change things?

What does this Surah teach us about bullying?

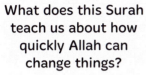

What does this Surah teach us about the importance of the Ka'bah and the respect we should have for it?

Let's Act

If we are ever in need of help or protection, let's ask Allah first, because without His help, nothing else matters.

The Quraysh
Surah Quraysh

Introduction

The first time young Muhammad ﷺ left Makkah on a trip was when he travelled in the summer to a far away land called Syria. He joined his uncle, Abu Talib, on a caravan packed with goods to sell in the busy markets of Syria.

Makkah's dry land made it difficult to grow food. So the Quraysh depended on these trips for almost everything, from grains and spices to fine fabrics, such as silk and wool. The Quraysh would travel to Syria every summer to trade with the people there. In the winter, they would go to Yemen to do the same. Their journeys were long and necessary.

But whenever the Quraysh returned safely to Makkah, they would thank the stone idols, forgetting their true Creator and Provider, Allah.

Young Muhammad ﷺ, however, never bowed to the idols or offered them thanks. Years later, when Muhammad ﷺ grew up as a man and became a Prophet, he was given a special Surah to remind the Quraysh about Allah's favour on their summer and winter travels.

Chapter 106
Surah Quraysh

      the One who gives mercy   The All-Merciful   Allah   With the name of

I start my recitation **with the name of Allah, the All-Merciful** to all of His creation, **the One who gives mercy** to the Believers.

(1)
of the Quraysh   For the comforting

For what Allah made easy in **the comforting of the Quraysh**.

(2)
and the summer   during the winter   of travelling   Their comfort

Their comfort of travelling in order to buy and sell **during the winter** in Yemen **and the summer** in Syria.

(3)
House   of this   the Lord   Then let them worship

Then since it is Allah who made travel comfortable for the Quraysh, **let them worship** Allah **the Lord of this House**, the Ka'bah.

Word-for-Word

and protects them — hunger — from — who feeds them — The One

(4) — fear — from

Let them worship Allah, **the One who feeds them** with all kinds of food and saves them **from hunger. And** Allah **protects them from** feeling any kind of **fear** during their journeys to Yemen and Syria.

DID YOU KNOW?

Surah Quraysh is the only Surah in the Quran named after a tribe. It is a reminder to the Quraysh to remember and worship Allah, especially because they were sent many special blessings from Him.

Firstly, the Prophet ﷺ is from the Quraysh. The first people on Earth to accept Islam were among the Quraysh, including great Sahaba like the Prophet's wife Khadijah, his best friends Abu Bakr, Umar and Uthman, and his beloved cousin Ali.

Even though this Surah was revealed about the Quraysh, we can all learn from it by thanking Allah for the special blessings we have.

Reflect Surah Quraysh

List some of the special blessings that Allah has given you.

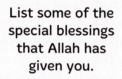

What does this Surah teach us about being grateful to Allah for the blessings we have?

How can we help others who don't have some of the same blessings as us?

What does this Surah teach all of us even though it only mentions the tribe of Quraysh?

What does this Surah teach us about how giving and merciful Allah is — even to those who don't thank Him?

Let's Act

Allah's blessings are all around us in things big and small. Let's always be thankful to Allah for everything He's given us.

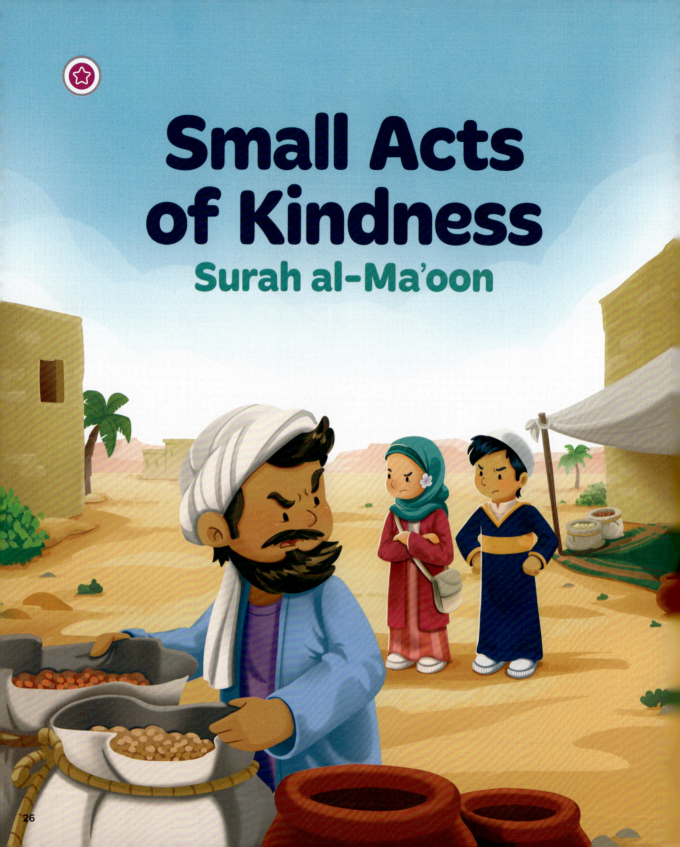

Introduction

In ancient Makkah, some young orphans were not looked after. The poor were left hungry, even while big feasts were prepared for those who were better off. This was how some of the leaders of Makkah behaved. They didn't believe in the Day of Judgement, when everyone will be asked about their deeds in this life. Without this belief, their hearts became hard and cold.

The Prophet Muhammad ﷺ taught the people of Makkah to care for the less fortunate. Years later, when the Prophet ﷺ moved to Madinah, he did the same there too. But just like in Makkah, there were a group of people who didn't care about being kind or helping others. This group wanted to appear as Muslims, so they acted like them on the outside. But deep down, they didn't believe in the Day of Judgement either. If they prayed or helped someone, it was not for Allah. It was just to show off so others would think they were good.

The Prophet Muhammad ﷺ was sent to the people of Makkah, Madinah, and the entire world to teach the message of the Quran. And in the Quran, Surah al-Ma'oon was revealed to let us know what happens if we forget the day when we will return to Allah.

Chapter 107
Surah al-Ma'oon

With the name of — Allah — The All-Merciful — the One who gives mercy

I start my recitation **with the name of Allah, the All-Merciful** to all of His creation, **the One who gives mercy** to the Believers.

1 — in the Day of Repayment — who does not believe — the one — Have you seen

Have you seen and wondered about **the one who does not believe in the Day of Repayment**, the Day of Judgement when people will be rewarded if they did good deeds and may be punished if they did bad deeds?

2 — the orphan — who pushes away — the one — That is

That kind of person **is the one who** has no mercy and **pushes away** instead of helping **the orphan**.

3 — the poor — feed — to — encourage (people) — And (he) does not

And that kind of person is so selfish that he **does not encourage** and tell people **to feed the poor** who need support and help.

Word-for-Word

And shame on those same kind of people **who pray Salah** without sincerity.

Those people in particular **who** do not **give their Salah proper attention** and delay the prayer or they don't pray properly.

Those same kind of people **who** only **want to be seen** praying with the rest of the Muslims because they like to show off even though they don't care about the Salah.

And they hold back and refuse to share even the **small things** like water and sugar with their needy neighbours and community.

29

Reflect Surah Ma'oon

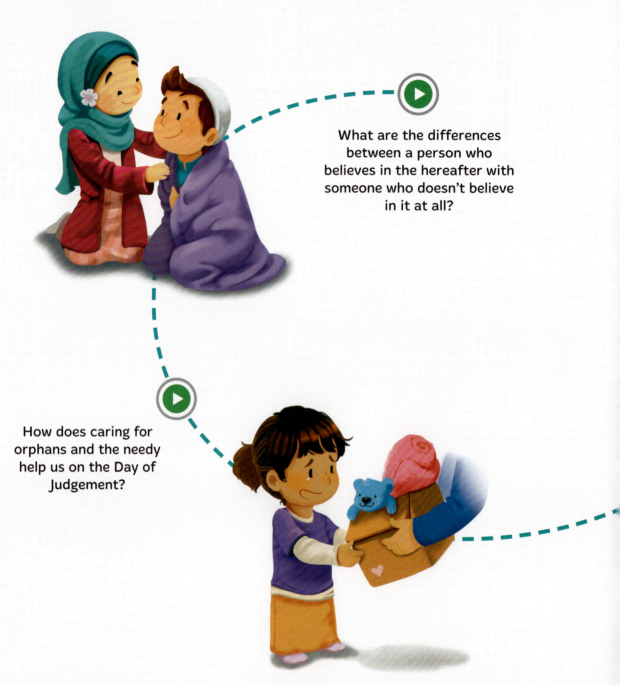

What are the differences between a person who believes in the hereafter with someone who doesn't believe in it at all?

How does caring for orphans and the needy help us on the Day of Judgement?

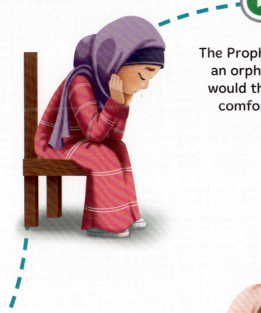

 The Prophet ﷺ was an orphan. How would this Surah comfort him?

 If someone does not share their small blessings with others, how likely are they to share some of their bigger blessings?

Let's Act

Let's always look to do a good deed, even if it's small. Allah loves those who are kind to others.

31

The Heavenly River
Surah al-Kawther

Introduction

When the Prophet Muhammad ﷺ first spread the message of Islam in Makkah, the people ignored him and did not listen. It was a very difficult time for the Prophet ﷺ. The people in Makkah were rude and their words were even harsher. Then, something heartbreaking happened. The Prophet's ﷺ young son passed away.

To the people of Makkah, having a son meant everything. A son meant strength, honour, and a name that would be carried on for generations. One cruel disbeliever named al-Aas bin Wa'il, saw the Prophet's ﷺ sadness and decided to make it worse. "Now that you have no son, your name will be forgotten. No one will remember you," al-Aas sneered.

But Allah, the Most Kind, saw the Prophet's ﷺ pain and sent down a powerful Surah to comfort him and remind him that he was never alone. Allah promised him a gift beyond anything anyone could imagine. It is a magnificent present, waiting for all those who love and follow the Prophet ﷺ. But as for those who tried to hurt him, they will be the ones truly forgotten and cut off from all goodness.

Chapter 108
Surah al-Kawther سُورَةُ الْكَوْثَرِ

the One who gives mercy • The All-Merciful • Allah • With the name of

I start my recitation **with the name of Allah, the All-Merciful** to all of His creation, **the One who gives mercy** to the Believers.

1 • al-Kawther • have given you • We

We have given you, O Muhammad, **al-Kawther** which is all types of good in this life as well as a special river in Paradise called al-Kawther.

2 • and sacrifice • to your Lord Allah • So pray Salah

So pray Salah and make du'a **to your Lord Allah and sacrifice** animals for His sake alone.

3 • cut off • (he) is • the one who hates you • Indeed

Indeed, the one who hates you and insults you **is cut off** from all kinds of good things in this life and the hereafter.

Word-for-Word

DID YOU KNOW?

One day, the Prophet Muhammad ﷺ was sitting with his Sahaba when he suddenly closed his eyes and fell asleep for a moment. He quickly woke up with a big smile on his face. "Why are you smiling, O Messenger of Allah?" The Sahaba asked curiously.

The Prophet ﷺ told them that a wonderful new Surah had just been revealed to him. He then recited, "We have given you al-Kawther…" Then he asked his Sahaba, "Do you know what al-Kawther is? It's a river my Lord has promised me. Its banks are lined with beautiful pearls, and its ground smells of pure musk."

The River al-Kawther will flow into a special pond called al-Hawd, where the Prophet's ﷺ followers will gather on the Day of Judgement. After they drink from the pond, they will never feel thirsty again.

But how will the Prophet ﷺ know who his followers are, if he's never met us? The Sahaba wondered the same thing, so they asked him.

"Just like a man can spot a horse with white marks among black horses, I'll recognise my followers by the brightness on their foreheads, hands, and feet from making wudu," the Prophet ﷺ responded. So, every time we make wudu for Salah, let's remember that these parts will shine brightly in front of the Prophet ﷺ at al-Hawd.

Reflect — Surah al-Kawther

What do the special favours mentioned in this Surah tell us about how much Allah loves and cares for His Messenger ﷺ?

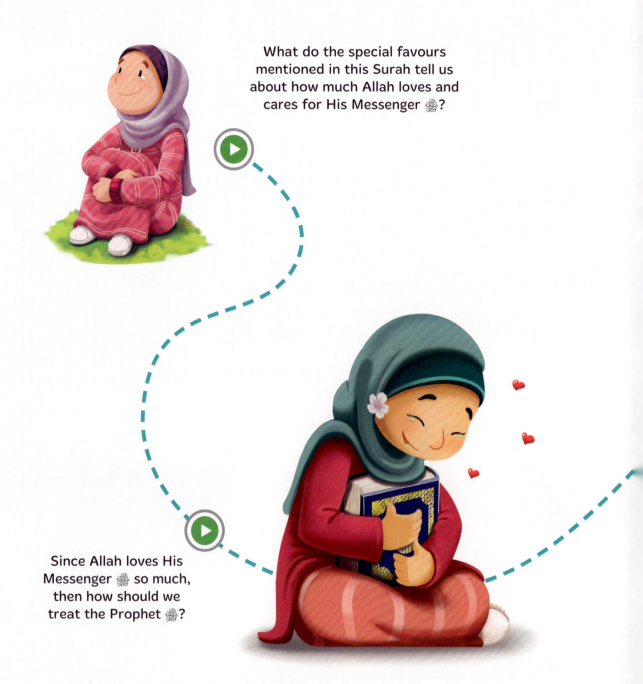

Since Allah loves His Messenger ﷺ so much, then how should we treat the Prophet ﷺ?

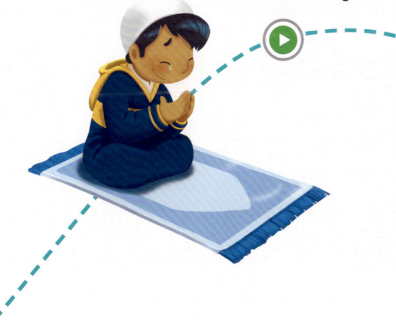

How important are Salah and sacrifice as ways for us to thank Allah for His blessings?

Let's Act

Let's not judge people by the amount of things they do or do not have. What really matters is how close they are to Allah.

Reflect on how comforted the Prophet ﷺ must have felt because Allah defended him. Now, describe how it feels to know that Allah cares and protects you too.

The Disbelievers
Surah al-Kafirun

Introduction

"Let's make a deal," a group of disbelievers said, coming to the Prophet Muhammad ﷺ. They thought they had a clever plan. Islam was spreading quickly in Makkah, and the disbelievers wanted to stop it before even more people could hear the message.

"We'll worship your Lord for a whole year, and the next year, you worship our idols," they said. They waited for the Prophet's ﷺ reply, thinking they had found the perfect way to slow down the message of Islam. But did they really expect the Prophet ﷺ to turn away from his beloved Lord, the One who created everything? Did they expect him to stop praying to the One who sees and hears all things, just to worship lifeless stones that could do nothing at all?

The Prophet ﷺ had always taught the Muslims to stand firm in their faith, no matter what happens. He had never bowed to an idol in his life, and he wouldn't worship one now or ever. He didn't respond to the disbelievers' offer. Instead, he remained silent, until Allah revealed a powerful Surah with the reply.

Chapter 109
Surah al-Kafirun سُورَةُ الْكَافِرُونَ

الرَّحِيمِ	الرَّحْمَٰنِ	اللَّهِ	بِسْمِ
the One who gives mercy	The All-Merciful	Allah	With the name of

I start my recitation **with the name of Allah, the All-Merciful** to all of His creation, **the One who gives mercy** to the Believers.

١	الْكَافِرُونَ	يَا أَيُّهَا	قُلْ
	disbelievers	O you	Say

Say, O Muhammad, **"O you disbelievers** who choose not to follow the religion of Islam.

٢	تَعْبُدُونَ	مَا	أَعْبُدُ	لَا
	you worship	what	do I worship	Never

Never do I worship what idols and false gods **you worship.**

٣	أَعْبُدُ	مَا	عَابِدُونَ	أَنتُمْ	وَلَا
	I worship	of what	worshippers	are you	And never

And never are you worshippers of what I worship which is Allah alone, the only true God.

Word-for-Word

And never am I a worshipper of what idols and false gods **you worship.**

And never will you be worshippers of what I worship which is Allah alone, the only true God.

For you is your religion of idol-worship **and for me is my religion** of Islam and worshipping Allah alone."

DID YOU KNOW?
The Prophet ﷺ taught us that reciting this Surah is a way of keeping away from shirk, which is to worship something or someone besides Allah. Shirk is the worst thing someone can do.

Reflect Surah al-Kafirun

From this Surah, what do we learn about the identity Allah wants us to have and protect?

How does the language used in this Surah emphasise its message?

What does this Surah teach us about respecting other people's choices?

Let's Act

Let's be the best example as Muslims, just like the Prophet ﷺ was. Many people did not believe in Islam until they saw his beautiful manners in action.

How do we follow the Prophet's ﷺ footsteps if people ask us to change our religion or do things which Allah is not pleased with?

The Victory
Surah an-Nasr

Introduction

More than 20 years had passed since the Prophet Muhammad ﷺ was sent by Allah to share the message of Islam. For many of those years, the Muslims struggled. At first, they kept their faith a secret. Later, when they told others about Allah, they faced even more hardship from the disbelievers.

Then came years of battles and challenges. People joined Islam, but mostly one by one. Then Surah an-Nasr was revealed, bringing wonderful news. Makkah would become a land of Muslims after being filled with idols. People would come into Islam in large groups, one after another.

But there was something that brought tears to the eyes of some of the Sahaba. They understood that if the Prophet Muhammad's ﷺ mission was almost complete, it meant he would soon return to Allah. It was a sad thought, but it certainly didn't mean the end of Islam. In fact, Islam would continue to grow and spread, even reaching us today. For this, Allah reminded the Prophet ﷺ and all the Muslims to praise Him, thank Him and ask Him for forgiveness.

Chapter 110
Surah an-Nasr

I start my recitation **with the name of Allah, the All-Merciful** to all of His creation, **the One who gives mercy** to the Believers.

O Muhammad, **when the victory of Allah** over your enemies **comes** to pass **and the conquest** of Makkah finally happens.

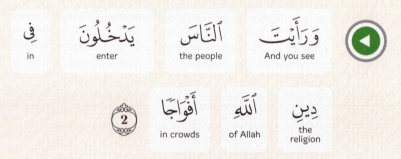

And you see the people enter and convert to **the religion of Allah** which is Islam **in crowds** of men and women, young and old.

46

Word-for-Word

Then your mission as a Prophet will be complete so **glorify your Lord with praise and seek His forgiveness. He is the One who accepts** repentance **from those who seek** His **forgiveness.**

DID YOU KNOW?
After Surah an-Nasr was revealed, our beloved Prophet Muhammad ﷺ often recited this du'a, especially in his prayers:

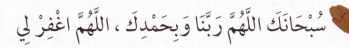

"How perfect You are, O Allah! Our Lord, and all praise is for You. O Allah, forgive my sins." (Bukhari)

When we accomplish something great, let's remember that we couldn't have done it without Allah's help.

Reflect Surah an-Nasr

Allah makes promises in the Quran. And no one is more true to their word than Allah. What effect do these promises have on the hearts of the Believers?

Describe how the Prophet ﷺ may have felt when hearing the news of people entering Islam in large numbers.

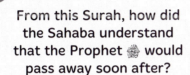

From this Surah, how did the Sahaba understand that the Prophet ﷺ would pass away soon after?

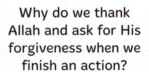

Why do we thank Allah and ask for His forgiveness when we finish an action?

Let's Act

Sometimes Allah decides to grant our wishes right away, and sometimes it can take more time. But either way, let's never lose hope of Allah's help, because He can do anything He wishes.

The Palm Fibre
Surah al-Masad

Introduction

The Prophet Muhammad ﷺ climbed Mount Safa, calling out to his family and tribe with a voice that reached all corners of Makkah. Allah had commanded him to start sharing the message of Islam with those closest to him. His family gathered around, ready to hear what as-Saadiq al-Ameen, the truthful, trustworthy one, had to say. The Prophet ﷺ told his people to leave their idols and worship Allah, the one true God.

In the crowd, one man's face grew dark with rage. It was the Prophet's ﷺ own uncle, Abu Lahab. He was not a kind or loving uncle. He was one of the fiercest enemies of Islam. He shouted at the Prophet ﷺ and stormed off, refusing to listen. Over the years, he did everything he could to stop the message of Islam.

Abu Lahab used his hands to hurt the Prophet ﷺ, thinking his money and power would protect him from getting into trouble. His wife would carry sharp thorns and scatter them in the path of the Prophet ﷺ, hoping he would step on them. As Islam grew and spread, so did their hatred. In response, Allah revealed Surah al-Masad.

Chapter 111
Surah al-Masad

| With the name of | Allah | The All-Merciful | the One who gives mercy |

I start my recitation with the name of Allah, the All-Merciful to all of His creation, **the One who gives mercy** to the Believers.

| 1 | and he is ruined | Abu Lahab | are the hands of | Ruined |

Ruined are the hands of Abu Lahab, the uncle of the Prophet Muhammad ﷺ who would bully him, **and he** Abu Lahab **is ruined**.

| 2 | he gained | or what | his wealth | to him | it be of any help | Never will |

Never will it be of any help in the hereafter **to him**, Abu Lahab, not **his wealth or what** children **he gained** in this life.

| 3 | blazing | in a fire | He will burn |

As a punishment for Abu Lahab's disbelief and evil-doing, **he will burn in a fire blazing** in Hell.

52

Word-for-Word

And as a punishment, **his wife** who also disbelieved and did evil, **will be made to carry fire-wood** for the fire of Hell.

Around her neck will be a rope made of twisted palm-fibres so she cannot escape the punishment she deserves.

DID YOU KNOW?

Surah al-Masad is a miracle Surah. In this Surah we learn that Abu Lahab would never accept Islam.

Abu Lahab could have pretended to accept Islam just to try and prove the Quran wrong. But he never did. He lived for almost 10 years after this Surah was revealed and stayed a fierce enemy of Islam.

Allah had destined that Abu Lahab would be in the fire, so he never believed. Because whatever Allah decides, will happen.

Reflect — Surah al-Masad

Reflect on how the Prophet ﷺ may have felt knowing that Allah was there to defend him. How do you feel knowing Allah is there for you too?

Abu Lahab's wealth and children will not help him on the Day of Judgement. But what will help a person on that special day?

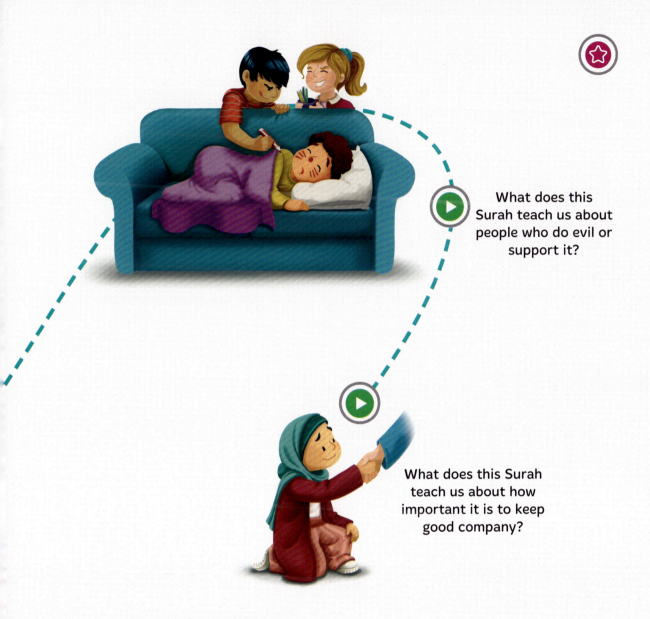

What does this Surah teach us about people who do evil or support it?

What does this Surah teach us about how important it is to keep good company?

Let's Act

Allah loves people who treat others fairly. So, whenever we meet people, let's treat them with kindness and respect.

Sincerity
Surah al-Ikhlas

Introduction

"Describe your Lord to us," said some of the disbelievers in Makkah to Prophet Muhammad ﷺ. They had spent their lives worshipping idols carved out of stone, moulded from clay, or even made of dates. To them, it was easy to worship these idols because they could see and touch them.

But the disbelievers didn't realise that they were the ones taking care of the idols, not the other way around. The idols couldn't even move or protect themselves. People had to clean them, carry them around, and carefully set them down so that they wouldn't crack or break.

Then after all that care, the idols couldn't listen to the disbeliever's prayers, help them in times of trouble, or even keep themselves safe. Now, the disbelievers wanted to know more about the God that Prophet Muhammad ﷺ was calling them to worship.

What they didn't expect was that the answer would come straight from Allah Himself, in the form of Surah al-Ikhlas.

Chapter 112
Surah al-Ikhlas

| the One who gives mercy | The All-Merciful | Allah | With the name of |

I start my recitation **with the name of Allah, the All-Merciful** to all of His creation, **the One who gives mercy** to the Believers.

| 1 | the One | Allah | He (is) | Say |

Say, O Muhammad, "**He is Allah, the One** true God who has no partners or equal.

| 2 | the One who does not need anything but everything needs Him | Allah |

He is **Allah, the One who does not need anything but everything needs Him.**

| 3 | was He born | and never | doe He have children | Never |

Never does He, Allah, **have children and never was He born** to any parents.

Word-for-Word

| | at all | anything comparable | to Him | is there | And never |

And never is there to Him anything in the creation **comparable at all** because He is unique.

DID YOU KNOW?

One day, the Prophet Muhammad ﷺ asked his Sahaba, "Could any of you recite one-third of the Quran in one night?" The Sahaba were surprised and wondered who could do that. The Prophet ﷺ then recited Surah al-Ikhlas, and said it is one-third of the Quran. (Bukhari)

By reciting this short but great Surah, we get the same reward as someone who recited one-third of the Quran!

With each recitation of Surah al-Ikhlas, we don't only gather great rewards, but we also add to an everlasting home in Jannah.

The Prophet ﷺ said that whoever recites Surah al-Ikhlas 10 times, "Allah will build for them a house in Jannah". (al-Jami' as-Saghir)

Reflect Surah al-Ikhlas

Everyone and everything needs Allah. But Allah does not need anyone or anything. Then why does Allah command us to worship Him?

How does believing and worshipping Allah alone make our lives better?

This Surah contains one of the most beautiful descriptions of Allah. How is Allah so different and unique compared to anything He has created?

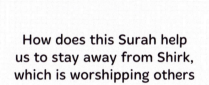

How does this Surah help us to stay away from Shirk, which is worshipping others besides Allah?

Let's Act

By reciting this Surah often, we can gather many great rewards. And since this Surah is short, it's easy to memorise and recite.

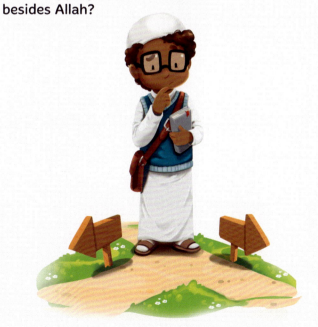

The Daybreak
Surah al-Falaq

Introduction

In Madinah, life was getting better for the Muslims. But not everyone was happy about it. Some of the people who did not believe in Islam were jealous of Prophet Muhammad ﷺ and wanted to hurt him. One of them even tried to cast a magic spell on him. To protect His beloved Prophet ﷺ, Allah revealed two powerful Surahs – al-Falaq and an-Nas – to protect and cure him from all harm.

In this world, there is good and bad. Not everyone is kind and not everyone wants good for us. There are also things that scare us, like creatures that come out in the dark or people who make us feel unsafe. Allah knows that we need His help to stay safe from things that worry or frighten us. Because no matter how bad evil gets, it can never escape Allah's power.

Just as Allah revealed Surah al-Falaq to protect the Prophet Muhammad ﷺ, we should also recite it to ask for His protection. Surah al-Falaq may be short, but its words are powerful. Let's discover its verses that, by Allah's will, guard us in ways we can't see or imagine.

Chapter 113
Surah al-Falaq

With the name of / Allah / The All-Merciful / the One who gives mercy

I start my recitation **with the name of Allah, the All-Merciful** to all of His creation, **the One who gives mercy** to the Believers.

1 / of daybreak / with the Lord / I seek protection / Say

Say, O Muhammad, "**I seek protection with** Allah who is **the Lord of daybreak**, the time when morning light appears after a night of darkness.

2 / He created / which / the evil of / From

From the evil of some of the creation **which He created**.

3 / it turns night / when / during darkness / the evil / And from

And from the evil things which happen **during darkness when it turns night**.

Word-for-Word

knots — into — those who blow — the evil of — And from

And from the evil of those witches **who blow** spells **into knots** in order to harm people with magic.

he envies — when — the envier — the evil of — And from

And from the evil of the envier when he envies the blessings which Allah gives some people but not others."

DID YOU KNOW?

Surahs al-Falaq and an-Nas are two special Surahs also called 'al-Mu'awidhatayn', which means 'the Surahs of asking for protection'.

Before they were revealed, the Prophet ﷺ would ask Allah for protection from evil things in different ways. But after they were revealed, he only used these two Surahs for protection. Reciting these Surahs is like putting on an invisible shield that keeps us safe from all kinds of harm, even things we cannot see.

Reflect Surah al-Falaq

What is special about the daybreak, such that Allah described Himself as the 'Lord of the Daybreak'?

What kinds of things happen in the dark, that we need Allah's protection from?

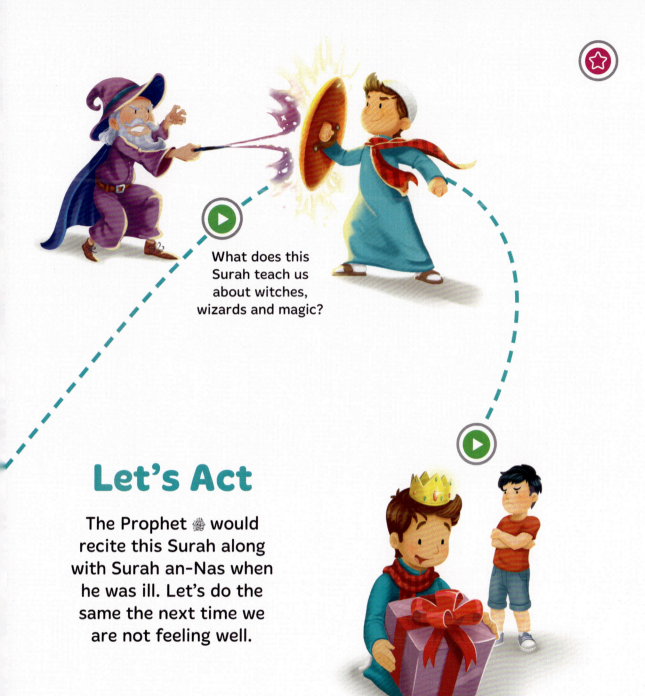

What does this Surah teach us about witches, wizards and magic?

Let's Act

The Prophet ﷺ would recite this Surah along with Surah an-Nas when he was ill. Let's do the same the next time we are not feeling well.

How can we protect ourselves from the evils of having envy towards others and from their envy towards us?

Introduction

Shaytan is a jinn who was commanded by Allah to bow down to Prophet Adam ﷺ. But Shaytan refused. He thought he was better than a human, and so, he was cast out of Jannah forever. From that moment onwards, Shaytan was filled with envy and anger towards humans. He promised to try his hardest to lead people to the wrong way by whispering bad thoughts to them.

Shaytan's whispers are sneaky. He tries to make us forget Allah and feel afraid, worried, or even unsure about doing what's right. And sometimes, there are even people who act like Shaytan, encouraging us to make choices that displease Allah.

Shaytan's whispers may be sneaky, but they are also very weak. By remembering Allah, Shaytan slips away, unable to reach our hearts. And the closer we stay to Allah, the further Shaytan stays away from us.

With Surah an-Nas, we remember that we never have to face Shaytan alone, because Allah is always there to protect us.

Chapter 114
Surah an-Nas سُورَةُ النَّاسِ

With the name of — Allah — The All-Merciful — the One who gives mercy

I start my recitation **with the name of Allah, the All-Merciful** to all of His creation, **the One who gives mercy** to the Believers.

Say — I seek protection — with the Lord of — all mankind — 1

Say, O Muhammad, **"I seek protection with** Allah who is **the Lord of all mankind,**

The King — (of) all mankind — 2

Allah who is **the King of all mankind,**

The God — (of) all mankind — 3

Allah who is **the** only true **God of all mankind.**

Word-for-Word

4 | who goes away | the whisperer | the evil of | From

From the evil of the whisperer Shaytan, who encourages people to do bad things but **who goes away** when they remember Allah.

5 | (of) all mankind | the hearts | in | whispers | Who

From the same Shaytan **who whispers** evil things and bad ideas **in the hearts** and minds **of all mankind**.

6 | and mankind | jinns | From

From the Shaytan and his gang who are from **jinns and mankind**."

DID YOU KNOW?
The Prophet Muhammad ﷺ would recite the last three Surahs in the Quran every morning, evening and before going to sleep so that Allah would protect him. Let's always remember to spend our day just like the Prophet ﷺ.

Reflect Surah an-Nas

Allah emphasises that He is our 'Lord', 'King' and 'God'. What message does this send to us as His creation?

Why is it important to seek protection in Allah from Shaytan's whispers?

Allah has given us many simple ways to turn to Him for protection. What does that tell us about Allah's care for us?

Shaytan runs away whenever we remember Allah. What does this tell us about Shaytan?

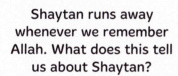

Let's Act

Let's make it a habit to recite this Surah every evening or before sleeping, so we can protect ourselves.

Alhamdulillah!

Together, we've learnt and reflected over the meanings and teachings of some of the shorter Surahs of the Quran.

Let's continue this learning journey with the Quran. The Prophet ﷺ said: **"It will be said to the one who recites the Quran, 'Recite and rise, just as you used to recite in the world. Indeed your level (in Jannah) will be at the last verse you recite'."**

(Musnad Ahmad)

LEARNING ROOTS

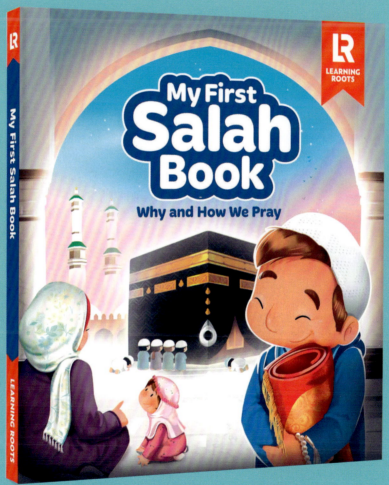

For the next level up, order online at:

LearningRoots.com

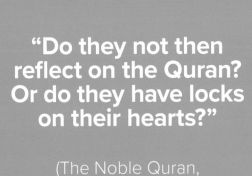

"Do they not then reflect on the Quran? Or do they have locks on their hearts?"

(The Noble Quran, Surah Muhammad, 47)